SOKAL

CANARDO

private eye

blue angel

Xpresso Books

a division of Fleetway Publications, Greater London House, Hampstead Road, London NW1 7QQ, a member

of Maxwell Consumer Publishing & Communications Ltd. UK Distribution and Export by MacDonald & Co

(Publishers) Ltd, Tel (071) 377 4600.

Steve Edgell

Editor

Frank Wynne

Translation

Rian Hughes

Cover Design

Michael W Bennent

Group Editor

First published in Belgium as La Mort Douce © 1981 Casterman

English Translation and UK edition © 1991 Xpresso Books

ISBN 1 85386 264 9

Printed and bound in the EEC

First edition September 1991

1 3 5 7 9 10 8 6 4 2

blue angel

FREDDO'S BAR

THIS IS IT...

ALEKSANDRA

SINGER REQUIRED APPLY WITHIN

MISTER FREDDO?

YEAH, THAT'S ME...

I'VE COME ABOUT THE JOB... I'M THE NEW SINGER...

HIC?

HA! HA! HA! SO YOU'RE TAKING OVER FROM ALEXANDRA...

?

YOU'D BE BETTER OFF FORGETTING ABOUT HER, CANARDO. THIS IS DOING YOU NO GOOD...

YOU MEAN YOUR LIQUOR IS DOING ME NO GOOD – DON'T MAKE ME FORGET A THING...

HA! HA! HA! HERE'S MUD IN YOUR EYE, KID!

DON'T PAY HIM NO MIND, LADY, HE'S JUST DRUNK!

COME ON, I'LL SHOW YOU YOUR DRESSING ROOM...

SO, WHAT'S THE MATTER WITH THE GUY?

UH ... THE LAST SINGER WE HAD DIED IN HIS ARMS ... HE HASN'T BEEN THE SAME SINCE.

... SHE WAS PRETTY ... I SUPPOSE HE WAS IN LOVE WITH HER ...

AAH, I TELL YOU, HE ALWAYS SEZ THAT ABOUT 'EM ONCE THEY'RE DEAD ... SO ...

ALEKSANDRA

... I'LL LEAVE YOU TO GET CHANGED... YOU'RE ON IN TEN MINUTES.

BAM!

KOF! KOF!

...AH, SHIIIT! NOT AGAIN!

LILI! ARE YOU OKAY?

AH, LEAVE ME ALONE, WILLYA!?

YOU CAN'T KEEP THIS UP, LILI... YOU SHOULD TAKE THE MEDICATION, IT MIGHT HELP SOME...

KOF! KOF!

HA! HA! HA! I JUST TOOK THE DAMN MEDICATION...

KOF! KOF!

FOR ALL THE DIFFERENCE IT MAKES...

... MEANWHILE, OUT IN THE RAIN...

FREDDO'S BAR

TONIGHT - LILI NIAGARA

2.

5

6

9

10

11

TWO HOURS LATER, AS DAY BREAKS...

BRONX? BRONX, IS THAT YOU?

HEH? AND WHO MIGHT YOU BE, HEH?

...A FRIEND... IN THEORY...

WHERE IS HE? WHERE'S BRONX?

...UH...

AN ACCIDENT? I KNEW IT! I JUST KNEW IT!

YOU SAID IT... BRONX KILLED SOMEONE IN THE VILLAGE LAST NIGHT...

HERE, I BROUGHT THIS... FIND IT'S PRETTY USEFUL WHEN THERE'S BEEN AN ACCIDENT...

HEH! HEH! WELL, SONNY, YER MOTHER TAUGHT YA MANNERS!!

...ALL THE SAME, POOR OL' BRONX... DUMB SHIT!

C'MON IN... IT'S A BIT CHILLY OUT HERE...

12

LATER...

THEN, SUDDENLY, HE JUST WENT MAD! MAYBE IT WAS BECAUSE OF LILI MARLEEN...

AH, I TOLD HIM! DIN'T I TELL HIM NOT TO MESS WITH WOMEN!!!

... IT'S NOT A WOMAN, JUST A SONG ...

AH!

BUT AFTER, HE RAN OFF WITH THE SINGER ...

OH!

... HADDA HAPPEN, I GUESS!

Y'KNOW, BRONX, HE'S JUST A DUMB ANIMAL. MOST O' THE TIME LIFE JUST GOES IN ONE EAR AND OUT THE OTHER ... AND THEN, SOMETIMES, SOMETHING STICKS ... AND SEEIN' AS THERE'S NOTHIN' ELSE IN HIS BRAIN, IT TAKES UP ALL THE SPACE ...

YEAH, BUT FOR A SONG TO MAKE HIS CORK POP LIKE THAT, MUST BE SOME WEIRD FREUDIAN SHIT!

HEH? WHUT'S THAT YOU SAID?

SOMETHING IN HIS PAST!

AHH, NOTHIN' COMPLICATED ABOUT HIS PAST. FOUND HIM WHEN HE WAS JUST A KID, I DID, DOWN BY THE RIVER, TIED UP IN THE REEDS BY THE BANK! WOULDA DIED THERE, TOO! SO, I TOOK HIM IN ... BROUGHT HIM HERE 'CUZ THERE'S NOTHIN' BUT SHIT DOWN BY THE RIVER - NOTHIN' BUT GARBAGE AND WRECKED CARS AND SWAMP! I WORK DOWN THERE MOST TIMES ... BUT THEN, I'M ON MY BACK MOST O' THE TIME ... NAH, I THOUGHT, FOR A MORON THE COUNTRY MIGHT BE BETTER ...

... SO, HE GREW UP HERE, THE BIG VEGETABLE... AND, Y'KNOW, I GOT TO LIKE HIM ... PRETTY MUCH ...

HMM, BETTER GO AND CHECK DOWN BY THE RIVER ... JUST IN CASE.

YE GOTTA BRING MY BOY BACK TO ME, HUH? I GOT WOOD NEEDS CHOPPIN' AN' I'M TOO OLD FOR THAT ... HIC! ... TH ... THANKS FOR THE LIQUOR ... HIC!

BRING HIM BACK ... YEAH, SURE! MURDER! KIDNAPPING! I GOT A FEELING BRONX'S REINTEGRATION INTO THE COMMUNITY WON'T BE SMOOTH!

10

SHIIIT... CHRIST, MY CHEST HURTS...

KOF! KOF!

WHAT THE HELL ARE WE DOING HERE? WHAT DID YOU BRING ME HERE FOR, HUH? TELL ME, SHITHEAD!

KOF! KOF!

HA! ... YOU DIDN'T FIGURE THAT, DID YOU, SMARTASS!? YEAH! I'M SICK! BUT I DON'T GIVE A SHIT ABOUT DYING, I JUST WANT SOMETHING TO KILL THE PAIN! DO YOU HEAR WHAT I'M SAYING, SHITHEAD?!

FORGET IT... I CAN DEAL WITH IT MYSELF. THERE HAS TO BE A SIGN OF LIFE SOMEWHERE IN THIS SHITHOLE!

ANYONE HOME?

BANG! BANG! BANG!

CAN ANYONE HEAR ME?!

14

NO GOOD LOOKING AT ME LIKE THAT, BRONX...

LOOK, IT'S YOUR FAULT... YA SHOULDNA KIDNAPPED ME LIKE THAT. YOU OWE ME ONE... ANYWAY, YOU'RE A BIG HEALTHY GUY, I FIGURE YOU GOT STRENGTH TO SPARE FOR ME... HUH?...

'COS I DON'T HAVE MUCH TIME LEFT... I'M NOT HAPPY, I'M NOT SAD... OR PRETTY OR UGLY... OR OPTIMISTIC OR BITTER... IT'S JUST... I'M LIKE A PLANT BUT I WANT TO BE A ROCK SO I DON'T HAFTA FEEL THE PAIN ANYMORE 'COURSE, IF I'M A ROCK I DON'T FEEL ANYTHING... IT'S A BITCH...

SO, I FIGURE THE BEST IS IF THE MACHINE STOPS. QUIETLY, SUDDENLY, WITHOUT TOO MUCH PAIN. MAYBE A LONG LIFE ISN'T THE BEST YOU CAN HOPE FOR *BUT A LONG DEATH IS SURE AS HELL THE WORST!!*

...HMM. IT'S EASY TO OPEN UP TO YOU... AT LEAST I KNOW THERE'S NO DANGER OF SCREWIN' UP YOUR HEAD. IT ALL JUST GOES IN ONE EAR AND OUT THE OTHER!

LATER...

YOU KNOW, THOSE ARE SOME PILLS! THE PAIN'S GONE AND I'VE STOPPED COUGHING...

YOU'RE GONNA WIN TONIGHT, AREN'T YOU? 'COS THAT WAY I CAN GET SOME MORE... HUH?...

20

21

YAHOO!! WE DID IT!

BRONX!

BRONX... YOU SCARED ME REAL BAD THERE...

...BRONX?

GIVE HIM A BREAK, KID... I THINK HE COULD DO WITH ONE. OR MAYBE YOU THINK HE SHOULD SAY THANKS FOR THE CUTS AND CONTUSIONS?

I...I JUST WANTED SOMETHING TO KILL THE PAIN... I... IT WAS THE ONLY WAY... SNIFF...

I'M A REAL BITCH, HUH? WELL, DON'T WORRY, I WON'T BE STICKIN' ROUND LONG...

...

...RECKON I CAN'T HOLD OUT MUCH MORE...

...SHEEIT!... SOME PARTY ANIMAL! LOOKS LIKE I'VE LANDED ME ANOTHER BLEAK, DIRTY-REALIST SCENARIO...

...C'MON. LET'S GET OUTTA HERE! THE DRINKS ARE ON ME!

HEY! THINGS ARE LOOKING UP!

HE'S RIGHT, KID! YOU DON'T WIN AT 30-1 EVERY DAY! COME ON, LET'S SEE IF WE CAN DROWN THAT VIRUS OF YOURS!

22.

...HIC! HIYA, GENERAL! MAKE A DEAL WITCHA. YOU COME AN' WALTZ WITH ME AN I'LL TELL EVERYONE YA GOT GREAT PECS!

?

HM... WELL...EH... 'IF IT WOULD MAKE YOU HAPPY, LITTLE LADY...

HA! HA! BRAVO, GENERAL! HERE, HAVE A DRINK BEFORE YOU GO INTO BATTLE!

...HELP YOU FORGET!

N-NOO!... CORPORAL KRONZ NEVER FORGETS. NEVER!!

WHO'S HE?

A DUMB SCHMUCK... LIVES WITH THE REST OF HIS KIND IN THE RUINS OVER THE OTHER SIDE O' THE RIVER... SPEND THEIR TIME PLAYIN' AT SOLDIERS. SECTION EIGHT, THE WHOLE LOT OF 'EM!

TWENTY YEARS THEY WAIT 'ROUND FER GOD KNOWS WHAT... AN' WHEN THEY RETIRE, THEY COME DOWN HERE TO DRINK AWAY THEIR VETERANS PENSION... DON'T LAST TOO LONG, MOST OF 'EM. SPEND THEIR TIME DRINKIN' AN' SCARIN' FOLKS WITH STORIES TO MAKE IT LOOK LIKE THEY AIN'T BEEN BORED ALL THEIR LIVES...

THEN, SUDDENLY, I SAW IT!! THE SHADOW OF ITS HUUUGE FIN TURNED HALF THE SEA AS BLACK AS NIGHT!!!

?

HA! HA! HIC! GO FOR IT, GENERAL! YOU'RE DRUNKER THAN I AM... HIC!

HEH! HEH! THIS GUY'S PRETTY GOOD!... MOST OF 'EM ARE BORING AS SHIT!

I CAN SEE IT, RIGHT UP BESIDE ME. I CAN SEE THE STEELY GLINT OF BLUE FROM ITS TEETH WHILE, FAR OFF ON THE HORIZON, AT THE END OF A BODY THE LENGTH OF A MILITARY PARADE, ITS GREAT TAIL CHURNED UP TIDAL WAVES IN A CALM SEA!!!

...ITS BREATH WAS A DENSE FOG ALL AROUND. YOU DIDN'T DARE PUT OUT YOUR HAND FOR FEAR OF LOSING IT!...

27

28

SHIIIT! ...MY HEAD! WELL, DON'T KNOW WHAT YOUR PLAN IS BUT MINE'S SIMPLE. I'M GETTING SOME SHUT-EYE!!

...'COS IT LOOKS LIKE IT'S GONNA BE A LONG DAY TOMORROW! I'D LIKE TO GET TO THE BOTTOM OF THE LILI MARLEEN MYSTERY. I NEED TO KNOW WHY IT DRIVES BRONX MAD BEFORE I TAKE HIM HOME.

HE'S RIGHT. AIN'T NUTHIN' ELSE TO DO: I'M GONNA GET ME SOME SHUT-EYE!

HMM ... YOU'RE A REAL PRO, HUH?

...LILI MARLEEN?!

GOOD NIGHT!

MMM...

ZZZ...

HEH! HEH! THEY'RE ASLEEP! TIME TO GET TO WORK!

SORRY, HONEY: IT'D BE A REAL SHAME TO BE HONEST WITH ALL THESE EASY PICKIN'S!!

ZZZ

ANYWAY,... I'VE GOT PLANS FOR YOUR BIG FRIEND. HA! HA! HA! GOOD OLD BRONX!

?

I KNEW IT! HE'S TRYING TO SKIP TOWN WITHOUT GIVING ME MY 'MEDICATION'!

JUST AS WELL THE DUCK CAME PREPARED FOR ANYTHING!

SNOOORE

FROM NOW ON, ALL I CARE ABOUT ... IS AN EASY DEATH ... WHAT ELSE CAN I EXPECT FROM THIS NASTY LITTLE SHOW ... ?

... IN THIS SHITTY COUNTRY, THE ONLY THING THAT'S GONNA CARRY ME OFF LIKE A GHOST INTO THE MIST IS THAT LITTLE ASSHOLE'S STASH ...

C'MON! GET IN, SHITHEAD! WHADDYA SCARED OF ?!

?!

BRONX! DON'T!

WHA ...?! QUICK, GET IN! DON'T PAY HER NO MIND!

?

DON'T GO WITH HIM, **BRONX**, HE'S A CHEAT, A THIEF! STAY **BRONX**. I REALLY LIKE YOU, Y'KNOW ...

WAP!

HA! HA! HA!

27.

31

OH SHIT! **LILI!!**

OOOH...

LILI? YOU OKAY? SAY SOMETHING FOR CHRISSAKE! WHO DID THIS TO YOU?

BRONX...

WES TOOK HIM... THEY WENT ACROSS THE RIVER.

OKAY, I'LL GO AND CHECK OUT THE FAR BANK...

KOF! KOF!

...YOU STAY HERE AND LOOK AFTER YOUR-SELF. YOU'RE SPLUTTER-ING LIKE AN OLD TRUCK!

LOOK AFTER MYSELF! HUH! EITHER HE'S REAL INNOCENT OR REAL DUMB! THE ONLY WAY I CAN LOOK AFTER MYSELF IS TO FIND **WES** AND HIS DOPE – AND **WES'S** THE OTHER SIDE OF THE RIVER!

SPLOOSH!

IT'S OKAY FOR HIM, A HERO CAN ALWAYS JUMP INTO A BOTTLE OR A RIVER TO FORGET HIS BROKEN HEART... AND CHRIST KNOWS THIS ONE'S NO TARZAN!

BUT EVERYONE KNOWS A HEROINE CAN'T GET BY WITHOUT HER HEROIN! HA! HA! HA!

SPLASH!

?

HEY! WAIT FOR ME!

SHIT! SHE'S NOT GONNA GET RID OF HER COUGH LIKE THAT!

30.

32.

36

THREE MINUTES LATER...

HEH! HEH! THINGS ARE PICKING UP!

KRAAK CLICK CLICK CLANG!

SHIT! WHAT DID YOU LET THEM LOCK US UP FOR?! YOU'VE GOT A GUN, YOU COULD HAVE...

I'M JUST CURIOUS. LOOKS LIKE BRONX ISN'T THE ONLY ONE WITH A SOFT SPOT FOR YOUR TORCH SONG... LET'S JUST SEE HOW THINGS GO...

KOF! KOF! KOF! KOF!

IT COULD TAKE A WHILE YOU SHOULD TRY AND GET SOME SLEEP.

KOF! KOF!

I... I CAN'T SLEEP. HURTS TOO MUCH...

LOOKS LIKE THERE'S A STORM BREWING...

KOF! KOF!

D'YOU...D'YOU THINK A BULLET IN THE HEART HURTS MUCH?

OH JESUS! HERE WE GO!

I...I COULDN'T DO IT MYSELF. BUT YOU COULD. WHEN I'M NOT EXPECTING IT... IT'S JUST...IT HURTS SO MUCH, Y'KNOW?

KOF! KOF! K... KOF!

PHEW! SHE'S PASSED OUT...THAT SHOULD GIVE YOU TIME TO GET YOUR STRENGTH UP AGAIN. YOU'RE GONNA NEED IT, KID! YOU CAN'T COUNT ON ME TO HELP YOU DIE...

I'M TOO MUCH OF A COWARD FOR THAT. AND ANYWAY, I'D HAFTA LIVE WITH IT, AFTERWARDS... IT'S NOT THE SORT OF THING YOU TELL YOUR KIDS...

THAT FIGURES... ONE LOOK AT THIS BUNCH OF SENILE BOY-SCOUTS AND I COULD HAVE TOLD YOU THAT...

NO WE ARE TO DIE TO BE PURGED OF A CRIME... A CRIME COMMITTED TWENTY YEARS AGO!

YOU SEE, WHEN WE WERE YOUNG, I, WITH MY OFFICERS AND A FEW SOLDIERS LEFT THE BARREN ISLAND IN THE SEA WHICH HAD BEEN OUR HOME... WE FELT OUR LIVES NEEDED DIRECTION, AND SO WE LEFT IN SEARCH OF MAN...

YEAH... STANDARD ANIMAL METAPHYSICS: ANIMAL SEEKS ANIMUS. WHO CARES?

AND HOW WE SEARCHED! A YEAR WE SPENT TOSSED ON THAT CRUEL SEA, FINDING AT LAST THE ESTUARY. WE NAVIGATED THE RIVER'S HOSTILE BANKS, AND, FINALLY, TWENTY YEARS AGO, WE CAME TO REST HERE... WITH ALL OUR WOES!!

...IN THESE BARRACKS, WE LIVED BY A RIGID DISCIPLINE; EVERY ACT, EVERY THOUGHT CENTRED ON ONE SUPREME AIM: TO WAIT FOR MAN!

... BUT THE EVENINGS WERE LONG AND WE NEEDED DISTRACTION... THERE WAS A BAR, FARTHER DOWN PAST THE RUINS, AND A GIRL WHO SANG TO LIGHTEN OUR ENNUI...

♪ VOR DER KASERNE ♪ VOR DEM GROSSEN TOR

... EACH OF US LOVED HER: MYSELF, MAJOR FASSBINDER, COLONEL THOMPSON AND... AND LIEUTENANT FRANZ VON STERNBERG!

WE WOULD HAVE DONE ANYTHING FOR HER: THOUGH IT MEANT BETRAYAL OR DESERTION... AND THEN... THEN SHE MARRIED LIEUTENANT FRANZ! ON THAT DAY, THE WORLD CAME DOWN AROUND US!!!

40

WE BEGAN TO HATE BOTH OF THEM. ONE EVENING, WE LURED **FRANZ** AWAY FROM THE BARRACKS ... WE KILLED HIM ... WE CONVINCED **MARIA** THAT **FRANZ** HAD DESERTED. SHE SAID NOTHING. BUT SOMETHING IN HER EYES CHANGED. AND THEN, ONE NIGHT, SHE WENT AWAY...

M ...MARIA ...

IT TOOK TWO YEARS FOR US TO FIND HER. SHE WAS LIVING IN SQUALOR IN THE WOODS BY THE RIVERBANK ... AND SHE HAD A **CHILD**!

WE WERE BESIDE OURSELVES ... WE HATED HER NOW AS ONCE WE HAD LOVED HER : MORE THAN LIFE ITSELF ! WE TORE THE CHILD FROM HER ARMS ! I SHOUTED AT HER : "SING ! SING FOR US! IF YOU STOP, EVEN FOR A MOMENT, I'LL CUT THE CHILD'S THROAT ! " ... AND SHE SANG ... ALL DAY AND ALL NIGHT, SHE SANG. THEN, AT DAWN, SHE COUGHED, HER VOICE STILL CLUTCHING AT THE GERMAN WORDS TO LILI **MARLEEN** LIKE A DROWNING MAN CLUTCHING AT STRAWS. SHE COUGHED AGAIN ... AND THEN SHE WAS SILENT ... SHE DIED OF EXHAUSTION ...

... MOMMY ...?

WE HAD BEEN DRINKING HEAVILY ... WE THREW THE CHILD, STILL BREATHING, INTO THE FREEZING RIVER ...

?

... AFTER THAT, NOTHING WAS EVER THE SAME ... IT WAS AS THOUGH A PLAGUE HAD VISITED THESE BARRACKS ! THE SOLDIERS DIED, ONE AFTER THE OTHER. THE BUILDINGS CRUMBLED. AND STILL WE STAYED HERE ! LITTLE BY LITTLE, WE REALISED WE WERE NO LONGER WAITING FOR **MAN**. WE WERE WAITING FOR THE HOUR OF JUDGEMENT. THE MOMENT WHEN OUR SIN WOULD BE EXPIATED. WE KNEW THAT **FRANZ AND MARIA'S SON WAS ALIVE** ! THAT ONE DAY WE WOULD PAY ! ... **WE WERE DOOMED** !

... IT'S ALL OVER ...

Y...YOU SHOULDN'T HAVE GONE OUT, *LILI* ... YOU'RE NOT WELL ...

KOF! KOF!

DO IT NOW, *CANARDO*... PLEASE ... I HAVEN'T A HOPE ANYMORE ...

I ... I DON'T KNOW WHAT YOU'RE TALKING ABOUT!

... KILL ME ...

K...K... AAAH *KOF!*

D... DON'T ASK ME, LILI ... PLEASE ...N...NOT THAT... ... *LILI* ...

AAAAAH!

N...NO...

...KOF...

45

XPRESSO BOOKS

Troubled Souls   *Garth Ennis and John McCrea*   £6.50

For a Few Troubles More   *Garth Ennis, John McCrea and Wendy Simpson*   £3.95

Canardo 1 – A Shabby Dog Story   *Benoit Sokal*   £4.50

Heart Throbs   *Max Cabanes*   £6.99

The Complete New Statesmen   *John Smith, Jim Baikie, Duncan Fegredo and Sean Phillips*   £7.95

2000 AD BOOKS

Anderson Psi Division: Shamballa   *Alan Grant and Arthur Ranson*   £5.99

Chopper: Song of the Surfer   *John Wagner and Colin MacNeil*   £5.95

Hewligan's Haircut   *Peter Milligan and Jamie Hewlett*   £4.50

The Judge Child Quest   *John Wagner, Alan Grant, Brian Bolland, Mike McMahon and Ron Smith*   £6.95

The Judge Dredd Mega-Collection   *John Wagner, Alan Grant and Ron Smith*   £6.95

Judge Dredd in America   *John Wagner and Colin MacNeil*   £5.99

Judge Dredd in Tale of the Dead Man   *John Wagner, Will Simpson, Wendy Simpson and Jeff Anderson*   £5.99

Sláine: The Horned God   *Pat Mills and Simon Bisley*

Volume 1   £4.50

Volume 2   £4.99

Volume 3   £5.95

DEFINITIVE EDITIONS

Judge Dredd – Bad Science   *Wagner, Grant, Mills and McMahon*   £4.50

Judge Dredd – Future Crime   *Wagner, Grant and Bolland*   £4.50

Judge Dredd – Hall of Justice   *Wagner, Grant, Mills and McMahon*   £4.50

Judge Dredd – Metal Fatigue   *Wagner, Grant, Bolland*   £4.50

If you have any difficulty obtaining these books, you can order direct from:

Fleetway Books, Lazahold Ltd, PO Box 10, Roper Street, Pallion Industrial Estate, Sunderland SR4 6SN. Tel (091) 510 8787.

UK customers please send a cheque or postal order. For postage and packing, on orders up to £5 add £1.20; on orders up to £10 add £2; over £10 add £3.50.

Overseas (excluding USA) and Eire customers please send either a cheque drawn on a UK Bank, an International Money Order or Bankers Draft in Sterling.

Postage and packing rates available on request.

All orders to be made payable to Maxwell Consumer Publishing and Communications Ltd. While every effort is made to keep prices steady, it is sometimes necessary to increase prices at short notice. Fleetway Books reserves the right to show on covers and charge new retail prices which may differ from those advertised here or elsewhere.